HOORAY FOR CANADA

HOORAY FOR CANADA

*Special Canadians talk about
what Canada means to them*

A CANADIAN LIVING PUBLICATION

Canadian Cataloguing in Publication Data

Main entry under title:
Hooray for Canada

Series of articles originally published in Canadian
living magazine.
"A Canadian living publication."
ISBN 0-9691959-1-5

1. Nationalism – Canada.

FC97.H66 1989   971   C89-090703-X
F1034.2.H66 1989

FC
97
.H66
1989 / 62,538

Telemedia Publishing Inc.
50 Holly Street
Toronto, Ontario
M4S 3B3

Printed and bound in Canada

NOVEMBER 1989

It has often been said that Canada has no national identity. Some Canadians view that as negative, suggesting we have a weak sense of ourselves in the world; others claim that having no single, absolute national identity is positive because it nourishes the cultural diversity within our borders.

It has also been said that if you asked half a dozen Canadians what Canada meant to them, you'd get six different opinions.

We were interested in exploring these diverse opinions and so we asked a group of well-known Canadians to express their feelings about Canada in a series of articles for *Canadian Living* magazine.

Their thoughts make fascinating reading. They're not the prepackaged ideas of image-makers. Neither are they the dusty words of history nor cliches of modern nationalism.

Their feelings for Canada are all very personal and rooted in very simple values.

In an overcrowded, impersonal and sometimes turbulent world, these writers talk about proximity to nature and a love of the land with all its many faces.

They talk about people, the importance of community and the enrichment of personal relationships.

They talk about a society where self-interest is still tempered with considerations for the common good.

And throughout all these articles runs a thread of gentility and quiet humor that is perhaps the ultimate proof of real conviction.

So we republish these articles with pride because we believe they contain the essence of identity and unity. And in real human terms, we believe they begin to explain why 27 million people who live within our shores have so much to be thankful for and wouldn't choose to live anywhere else.

Robert A. Murray
Publisher, *Canadian Living* magazine

CONTRIBUTORS

Harry Bruce
Author and freelance journalist,
president of Bruce Communications
Limited, Guysborough, N.S.

June Callwood
Author and columnist for *The Globe
and Mail*

Carol Ferguson
Founding food editor of *Canadian
Living* and *Canadian Living's FOOD*
magazines

Peter Gzowski
Author and columnist, host of CBC
Radio's "Morningside"

Michele Landsberg
Author, award-winning journalist and
columnist for the *Toronto Star*

Roy MacGregor
Author, columnist for the *Ottawa
Citizen* and winner of four National
Magazine Awards

Alice Munro
Short story writer and three-time
winner of the Governor General's
Literary Award

Hartley Steward
Vice-president of the Toronto Sun
Publishing Corporation and publisher of
the *Ottawa Sun*

CONTENTS

HOORAY FOR CANADA

Once Upon a Prairie Childhood

Carol Ferguson

his country is a many-splendored gift. It's like one of those enormous, alluringly wrapped packages that, when opened, reveals another even better inside, then another and another, until you get to something very special at the centre.

Every nook and cranny of Canada is a gift-feast for the senses. It offers us a bounty of flavors at our tables, a colorful tapestry of literature and art, incredible natural beauty and vast, quiet spaces. And, best of all, the wings to fly and eyes to see it all. My country calms me and excites me, comforts me and delights me. I'm passionately nationalistic and hopelessly romantic about it. This is especially so when I'm on the Prairies where I was born. But since I'm always being told that I over-romanticize my roots, I'm going to talk first about perogies.

Last evening, as I slid some frozen poly-bagged perogies (imported from Saskatoon) into a microwave dish (according to package directions), I contemplated how far we've come (or gone, depending on how fussy you are about perogies). My Toronto supermarket stocks them regularly now, alongside the croissants and phyllo, pizza crusts and wonton wrappers. And I hear that they've recently appeared in trendy California restaurants as the hottest new "foreign food." But as ethnic foods go, perogies have been slow to make their debut.

Until recently, to get a really good home-cooked perogy, you had to be Ukrainian or get invited to a big wedding in Winnipeg or Edmonton. Over the years, I've devoured a goodly number of the delectable little dumplings, but even though I grew up in Humboldt, a Saskatchewan farm town surrounded by some of the best perogies in the West, I never actually tasted one until I was in high school. During the province's 50th birthday celebrations in 1955, our town held a heritage festival (the first ever, as I recall). The district's multicultural mix of pioneer roots was represented with dancing, singing and especially food – a whole hall of mysterious things I'd never seen, smelled or tasted before. It was a revelation. I still remember my sudden awareness of what had been around me all my life – German, Ukrainian, Polish, Yugoslav, Scandinavian, Jewish, Chinese (along with a kilted few of my own kin) – and my astonishment at how deliciously interesting were the *paskas* and strudels, *holubtsi* and perogies. How was it possible not to know about these?

It was just the way things were then. Fifty years is not very old for a province, especially for one that grew from a vast and largely uninhabited territory of unbroken prairie. In 1955, the original homesteads were still vivid memories for many people. They had survived the hardships, the blizzards and the loneliness by sheer determination and by sharing what they could, including food. They ate what was put in front of them, and culinary fashion was the last thing on their minds. Even when they managed to acquire the ingredients to reproduce the beloved dishes of their homelands, the old-country heritage was rarely romanticized. Survival was the thing, and the sharing of ethnic diversity was a luxury that would wait for a while. Even by the mid-'50s, we children of immigrants had little sense of local history. I remember being vaguely aware that my hometown was named after someone called Alexander von Humboldt and that it was near the historic Carlton Trail, but we really didn't know where we had come from until long after we had left.

As I was growing up on my mom's good British cooking, I remember a lot of sharing of recipes among her friends. But even though the poppy-seed cake from Mrs. Sawatsky next door was German in origin and the *pyrizhky* came via a Ukrainian neighbor, there was no real curiosity about their origins. For the most part, the ladies in church and tea circles all served up the same dishes and baked all the same goodies: cinnamon buns, lemon tarts, date squares, Saskatoon pies and cream puffs – the classic Prairie baking that remains entrenched today, even as each decade introduces more and more new tastes to Prairie palates.

It wasn't until my university days in Winnipeg that I moved on to an awareness not only of ethnic foods but also to the interwoven stories of the people who brought them here. Winnipeg was older than my hometown, and its turn-of-the-century roots were beginning to show. Of the million immigrants who passed through the city on their way west in the early 1900s, enough stayed to plant the seeds of many cuisines. As distinctive neighborhoods grew and flourished, so awareness of, and fondness for, individual cuisines increased.

By the 1920s, things were looking up on the rest of the Prairies, but the Depression, and later the Second World War, intervened to cut the gastronomic good times short. It took two more decades before enough affluence and foreign travel, plus a second great wave of immigration, turned Canadians into celebrators of gastronomic diversity. My generation watched that turning of our tables.

And so, our children are different. By the early '70s, my kids' public school in suburban Toronto was a mini-United Nations. Their Christmas concerts were a joyful jumble of languages, costumes and wonderful things to eat. Their ears and eyes and taste were attuned very early to a very large world, and lots of travelling reinforced their culinary open-mindedness. They grew up streetwise and liberal and cooking Italian, French and Jamaican.

There's no country more diverse than ours. At 5,200 kilometres wide, from east to west, Canada has such a variety of regional geography, climate, history and life-styles that it's incredible it holds together at all. It may sound trite to say (and I've said it so often) but our food provides one of our strongest ties. Canadians love to commune across their tables. Our local food styles represent the spirit our country was founded on – maintaining individual identity while sharing the whole. If that's overly romantic, I don't care. It's a wonderful country, gentle and strong, proud and free, and anyone who doesn't feel that is missing a lot. I am enraged by Canadians who whine about their country and want to split it up; they need to pull up their chairs to each other's tables. They need to look both farther and closer instead of fussing myopically in the middle. No Canadian could remain cold-hearted after a good honest Prairie farm dinner or a Newfoundland "scoff."

My own mind's eye wanders over a memory album of images that never fail to make me feel unabashedly happy to be Canadian.

☐ looking out at the sea from the easternmost point in North America as an old fisherman told me that his family's ancestors were Newfoundland-born for so many generations he had no idea where they originally came from;

☐ on a fishing boat off the west coast of Vancouver Island, gazing across another vast seascape, savoring a Japanese-Canadian fisherman's salmon sushi;

☐ summertime in Toronto, my city of delicious neighborhoods, sidewalk cafes and the best lemon gelati outside of Rome;

☐ from my highrise hotel window, a wide, wide strip of sunrise over winterbound Winnipeg, a city so solid and comfortable with itself. And then, down on the street, the fragrance of Viennese coffee over chess games in an old-world cafe;

☐ the same hotel view on a sizzling summer evening, a skyful of sunset after a day sampling Scottish at Lower Fort Garry, Icelandic at Gimli, Mennonite at Steinbach and French at St. Malo, where Normand's Cafe sign declares Our Cooking's So Good You'll Think We Kidnapped Your Mother;

☐ in southern Saskatchewan, my grandmother's old farmhouse, empty now in the middle of a wheat field but filled for me with images of my gentle granny pouring tea, a crowd of cousins around the big dining table, the fragrance of lilacs and sweet peas, a hot summer breeze billowing the curtains of my upstairs bedroom. The overgrown garden still holds the summer heat of the strawberry patch, and the shade trees around the edge evoke the laughter of my uncles swapping stories at our big family picnics.

Such gatherings took place everywhere on the Prairies; socializing over good food sustained the bonds of families and neighbors and nourished their common identity. But the Prairies also produce a strong strain of individuality in its sons and daughters. Prairie people spend a lot of time alone, and that makes them very free-spirited.

I always think of my father when I return to the Prairies. Last summer, as I wandered about southern Saskatchewan, in the rolling ranchlands and badlands of the Big Muddy Valley, my father's stories came rushing back to me, his voice leading me through the coulees, past salt lakes and along back roads. Now and then a ghostly dance hall, railroad station or grain elevator would emerge to match exactly the old photographs I carried with me; at other times it was simply the touch of the wind, the scent of sagebrush or a long-abandoned trail across the hills that spoke to me. Mostly, it was just me and that enormous sky, as it had been for my father, alone and free inside a full circle of horizon and the sound of silence.

"Who do you think you are?" is a common Canadian attitude that often gets in the way when we try to define ourselves. We seem to prefer the neutral, the understated approach. Prairie people, especially, have no patience with people who put on airs. But they are, at the same time, some of the world's greatest romantics (when romanticism is defined as freedom of spirit and feeling). Their environment breeds a soul-attachment to the land, a special kind of love. And they know that identity seekers, like lovers, sooner or later need silence. There are no words, will never be the right words, to define ourselves. Quietly, quietly, we know who we are.

Peter Gzowski's Canadians

When *Canadian Living* asked "Morningside" host Peter Gzowski to write about his favorite Canadians for our "Hooray for Canada!" series, he loved the idea but was poised at his computer, ready to write the final draft of his new book, *A Private Voice: A Journal of Reflections.* "Maybe later," he promised.

We were disappointed. We wanted Peter to share his wonderful anecdotes about Canadian people from his years as a radio host, editor, writer and insightful commentator on Canadians and Canadian life. More than that, we wanted to hear what Peter had to say about celebrating Canada because he does it best. Every day on radio, he makes us feel proud. His passion and respect for things Canadian spill over the airwaves and magically, through him, we talk to each other and discover how much we share and how alike we are all the way from Victoria to St. John's, Nfld.

Needless to say, we were delighted when he called us back, after completing his book, to say, "I think I have exactly what you want in my book."

His memoirs as he tracks his career over the years are as warm, honest, personal, funny and irreverent as you'd expect from him. But throughout the pages, there's also a quiet nationalistic trumpeting. And his enthusiasm is infectious. When he announces what makes him a Canadian and not an American, we agree.

"I like the Queen," he writes, "(though not as much as the Queen Mum) and am content to have her representative as a head of state. I like the ceremonies that spring from our royal tradition, too

... I know how to plug in a car at night and how to pronounce 'slough'. ..."

And although he was raised in Ontario, like so many other Canadians he feels that other parts of the country are home to him, too. He's rather proud that some people think he comes from Saskatchewan, which he calls "the most Canadian of provinces." "People who have listened to me on the radio have told me they were convinced I came from the Prairies," he says. "I'm never sure why this should be. . . . Whatever the reason, the misconception pleases me, as it proves that I learned something while I was there."

What follows are Gzowski's Canadians: people he has interviewed, people he remembers and the others, people who are very special to him.

Trudeau sipped water; I drank Scotch
So much of what has attracted our professional attention over the years has concerned this man. I wrote about him in *Maclean's* in my year in Montreal. Even then, he seemed set apart from other people, as if his mind was set on more important things. He was disconcerting to interview. As part of my preparation for writing about him, I showed up at his mother's house in Outrement at 10 in the morning. "Want a drink?" he said, and I, fresh from Toronto and thinking what a risque bunch these French Canadians were, accepted. He poured me three fingers of Scotch, then sat sipping water under the original Braque on the mantelpiece, looking owlish as I drank myself stupid.

Welcome to Canada, Citizen Carmen
The Ivan barbershop (formerly Mr. Ivan's), downtown Toronto, 2:30 p.m.: Carmen, the star of the Ivan, is one of the constants in my kaleidoscopic life. He has been cutting my hair for 10 years, ever since CBC television stopped paying for it. He has seen me through four books, a lot of hangovers, love, separation, the birth of my granddaughter, Stephanie – of all of my friends, he understood the pleasure best – and the evolution of my beard, which he refused to scoff at in its youth ("Looks nice, Mr. Peter.") and which he came into "Morningside" to shave off, live, on the radio, when the Edmonton Oilers won their first Stanley Cup. He is a stocky, smiling man, unfailingly good-natured, but respectful of his clients' private

moods. If you want to admire the multihued parade of beauty that passes by his window on summer mornings, a symbol of the changing face of the city, he joins in your appreciations. But if you don't want to talk, he works silently. He wears a shirt and tie, uses steaming towels and pungent lotions, trims your beard with a straight razor, and rubs your shoulders with a vibrator. Every couple of weeks, I make an appointment with him. Ritualistically, I inquire after the progress of his daughters through school, deplore the state of the Maple Leafs or the Blue Jays, celebrate the triumphs of Italian soccer and Stephanie's latest achievements, and fall asleep under his ministrations. My hour with him – he will not be rushed – is an hour of peace.

Today, he has become a citizen. The customer before me, he says has told him he'll have to cheer for Canada in the World Cup, and drink Canadian wine. He is beaming. "When you get home tonigh', Mr. Peter," he says, "ask you girlfriend if you look any differen'. Tell her you hair-a cut by a Canadian."

Unlike me, Don Harron is nicer in person than on radio
Don is as complex a man as walks the earth, a living proof of the theory that Canadians can express their humor only from behind masks. The corny, frequently naughty malapropisms of his best-known character, Charlie Farquharson, the double entendres of his waspish Valerie Rosedale, the lightness of his lyrics for Anne of Green Gables, all disguise the workings of a restless and reflective mind. Like many great comedians, he can be as melancholy in person as he is mirthful on the stage, but – as someone who worked with us both once pointed out to contrast him with me – he is, if anything, more pleasant away from the microphone than he is on it.

We're blessed with Pierre Berton – and a little jealous of him
Pierre Berton is in the "Morningside" studio to talk about his new book. Pierre's presence means I've won this season's fight with Gloria [Bishop, who was the executive producer] – and, to be fair, with a lot of the other producers as well. We have the same squabble, or so it seems, every fall. Pierre brings out a book – always in September, since he believes in getting a jump in the race for the best-seller lists. I say let's do it; he's one of the great talkers, always interesting. They say let's not; he's overexposed. So far, I've won most of the battles, though sometimes at a price. One year, at least in

part as overreaction to the office feeling, I was uncharacteristically aggressive with him. It was over his book-length essay, *Why we act like Canadians*. I lit into him, saying, for example, that his thesis about our having made peaceful settlements with the aboriginal Canadians didn't take into account the slaughter of the Beothuk, and that he hadn't done justice to Quebec. He defended himself well enough, goodness knows – he thrives on that sort of challenge – but a lot of people, including Elsa Franklin who looks after his book promotion, were taken aback by my belligerence.

People, probably including my colleagues, assume Pierre and I are friends. Not so. In the nearly 30 years since we overlapped at *Maclean's*, I've run into him dozens and dozens of times. I've read him, interviewed him, been down the bench from him at "Front Page Challenge" (a game he takes more seriously, by the way, than Nancy Howard takes horse-racing) and occasionally sought his counsel. But I've never spent more than a few minutes alone with him when he was not on display. I think, for what it's worth, that he is an absolutely stunning genius of the craft we both practise, an eloquent writer, an insatiable reporter, a compelling anecdotalist. Whatever the academics make of his works of history – and surely at least a few of them have been a tiny bit jealous – I also think we have been blessed that he has turned his eye to our past, and that for generations to come we will be grateful to him. It bothers me no end that, in our curious Canadian way, we have elected him to prominence and then, from time to time, criticized him for the very stature we have awarded him – or, as even my own producers do, begrudged him his prolific output. (I once asked Wayne Gretzky if, having been so celebrated so early, he feared a later reaction – the same thing that happened to Berton. Wayne, bless his heart, said "Is Pierre Berton a Canadian?")

I hit if off with what's-his-name, the lieutenant-governor of Saskatchewan
The last event of this part of my tour to promote *The New Morningside Papers* – my travel has all been built around it, in fact – is my second dinner for the Writers' Development Trust, and now, bedecked in the dinner jacket I've toted for the occasion, I stand in a receiving line for the 200 people who've paid to eat buffalo steak and hear me speak. I'm surrounded by dignitaries.

On my left [at dinner] is Mrs. Grant Devine – Chantal, as everyone at the table calls her (a custom I have easily adopted), a

prepossessing *bilingue* from Gravelbourg. On my right: the lieutenant-governor, a former chief justice of the province (I learn) who is
splendidly suited for his current appointment. Over the buffalo and
the blueberry pucks, His Honor has talked movingly of his love for
the country, which he has explored from Cape Spear to Long Beach,
of his views on the Constitution and of – he looked slyly around the
room before he said this, noting the presence of the owners of several
private stations – his affection for the CBC. The Queen's representative and I, in fact, are getting along like a house on fire.

As Grant Devine rises to introduce me, the lieutenant-governor
makes a flattering gesture to me. He picks up a copy of *The New
Morningside Papers*, which, along with some books by the Saskatchewan writers at the dinner, has been left at the table, and asks if I will
sign it for him as a memento of the evening. Rather proudly, I reach
for a pen.

And suddenly realize I have a problem. The question, class, is:
What is the name of the lieutenant-governor of Saskatchewan?

I can't believe I don't know it. Surely, when I was introduced to
him before in the receiving line. No, that was "Your Honor, may I
present ..." and all through dinner I've just been saying "Your
Honor," this, "Your Honor," that.

Chantal? Too late to ask her now. At the podium, her husband is
almost finished a surprisingly warm introduction and preparing to
leave for a later engagement.

I brandish the pen, as if trying to muster an appropriately
sincere dedication – which, come to think of it, I am.

His place card! I peer past his coffee cup as he beams in
anticipation. It's lying on its face.

The premier finishes and begins to make his exit.

I write: "To His Honor – a great Canadian, Regina, Saskatchewan, November 6, 1987."

The lieutenant-governor of Saskatchewan, by the way, was the
Hon. Frederick William Johnson, BA, LLB, etc.

Evelyn Hart is on my list of the 10 best things
On my list of the 10 best things in the world:
☐ Homemade strawberry ice cream (Gill and I have a Donvier
ice-cream maker which I swear by; the secret is to use all whipping
cream);

☐ Sable Island (I was there in the summer of 1986, filming a television program that was never shown);

☐ Roger Angell writing about baseball in *The New Yorker*;

☐ Gas barbecues (I scarcely cook with anything else at the cottage);

☐ Hand-knit socks;

☐ September (a reflection of my own good mood these days, I'm sure, and the golden days at Lake Simcoe);

☐ Shirtwaist dresses (I had to call Patsy Pehleman at home to ask what "those simple dresses with collars" were really called);

☐ The ballerina Evelyn Hart (whom I had met and been enchanted by, both on and off the stage);

☐ Newly talcumed babies (ah, Stephanie, my perfect granddaughter, whom I saw briefly at the end of the summer when Maria and her husband, Scott, brought her to the cottage);

☐ and "Over the Rainbow," which I substituted at the last minute for Ian and Sylvia's original version of "Four Strong Winds," and which Dave Amer [music director for "Morningside"] played on the radio, by Judy Garland, when I finished reading.

You can't win them all

I wrote down the eight most difficult interviews I had ever done on "Morningside," and read the list on air. They were:

☐ Martin Short, whose wife, living in Toronto. was a fan of the program and urged him to accept our invitation when he was in town but who turned out to be as pedestrian in conversation as he can be hilarious on television;

☐ Betty Friedan, who, from our Ottawa studio one day, assumed I was an enemy of her cause and shouted hostility at me no matter what I said (I was later told she was hard of hearing);

☐ Mordecai Richler, who, in spite of – or perhaps because of – our friendship, refuses always to respond to any question to which he knows I know the answer, and inevitably turns the tables on me with unbridled glee ("I have your picture over my bed," he said once after an embarrassing poster had been released by the CBC, "right next to Boy George.");

☐ Northrop Frye, for reasons I've already explained in this journal. [He answers the question posed, which means he frequently says only yes or no.];

☐ Ray Hnatyshyn, who as minister of justice, replied to my questions on the Tories' censorship bill in impenetrable political circumlocution;

☐ Mavis Gallant, who, while good, if superstitious, company at the race track where I took her one day when she was writer-in-residence at the University of Toronto, in public conversation makes me feel stupid;

☐ Shirley MacLaine, who is as solemnly wacky in person as her books and not much fun;

☐ and a woman named Elvira Lount, who came in one day, dressed like a Queen Street gypsy, to promote a film about her great-uncle Samuel Lount and turned out to know somewhat less about him than I know about how to hit a golf ball straight.

June Callwood is the queen of writers

June Callwood and Bill (her husband, Trent Frayne, but no one who has known them as long as I have calls him Trent) are yet two more friends who go back to my early days at *Maclean's*.

Before she became an activist, June was not just a magazine writer. To those of us around *Maclean's*, which is where she was selling most of her stuff, she was *the* writer: astute in concept (she was the first person in North America to write about thalidomide, to take just one example), painstaking in research, elegant in style. There were others who could do individual pieces better, perhaps, but fact for fact and phrase for phrase, Callwood was the queen. So one of my first acts, when I was given the assignment to write about Ross McLean [one of the pioneers of CBC television, now deceased] was to visit her. Formally, I wanted to talk about Ross's background in Brantford, Ont., where they'd known each other as teenagers. But more crucially, I wanted advice on how to write a profile.

I don't remember any of the anecdotes she gave me, but I do remember what she said about writing about people who worked in similar fields to your own and whom you'd be likely to see again. "You'll be very aware," she warned me, "that if you write about someone like Ross, he's going to read it. You can't help thinking about that; you'll see him looking over your shoulder. But you must ignore it – you have to. You have to forget about your friends."

We flash forward now, from the late 1950s to the early '70s. I am hosting "This Country in the Morning." June is writing a column in the *Globe*, called "The Informal...," and after a couple of seasons, I qualify to be a.... She comes to see me at the CBC, and we talk into her tape recorder for about an hour. Three weeks later, her portrait of me appears. It is, as I should have expected, brilliant: tough – heartachingly so, if being accurate is being tough – but also gentle and affectionate and, in the end, fair; by far the closest anyone has yet come to capturing me in print.

I don't see her for several weeks after that. Then one day she is at the CBC again, picking up a cheque. I scurry over to say how much I appreciated the piece, toughness and all.

"Thank heavens," she says. "I had a terrible time writing it. I was so conscious of you looking over my shoulder I couldn't even get started."

I may not be hip but I'm not as bad as Mordecai

I wish Daniel Richler [Mordecai Richler's son] had been stronger, though it's not his fault. "Morningside" has been trying to find a way to cover the music, films, fashion and trends young people are talking about almost as long as I've been here. It came up again – and eyes rolled – at our meeting at the cottage [Gzowski's cottage in Sutton, Ont.] last month. The trouble has always been that the people who know about it and take it seriously have always presumed so much knowledge on my part that they lose me before they get rolling; they want to comment on what I need explained. Daniel was to be the solution. To keep his expectations of my prior knowledge low, I told him to try to think of talking to me on the air as making things clear to his father. ("90 Minutes Live" once flew Mordecai to Halifax, along with Daniel's youngest brother, Jacob, so Mordecai could read *Jacob Two Two Meets the Hooded Fang* on television. We kept them around when their segment was finished, and brought out the evening's featured singer, who happened to be Bruce Murray. "He's Anne Murray's brother," I said. "Who's Anne Murray?" Mordecai asked.)

Sometimes it's easier to be intimate on radio than face-to-face

My head is down. Sign, sign, sign. "Is that Anne with an '*e*'?" "And what's your mother's name?" "You're doing your Christmas shopping early, aren't you?"

I come to a stop, however, when a strikingly attractive young woman – I look up for *some* things – presents a copy of the book, opened to the middle of my introduction, her thumbs bracketing a particular phrase.

"I'm Joanne," she says.

It takes me a minute, but the phrase she has framed is the clue.

In December 1985, we had an unusually large response to a drama about adoption, and in the weeks that followed, carried a number of personal letters and interviews based on it. After Susan Rogers and I – Susan produced the series – both thought we had rung every change on the theme, we learned of a moving incident. A woman in Northern Ontario, who had heard the piece we did with an adopted child explaining how deeply she would like to meet her birth mother, decided, 22 years after the fact, to search for her own daughter. With some difficulty, she found her, and because of the involvement of "Morningside" in the story, agreed to talk with her by studio link, Sudbury to Ottawa with me, gulping back my emotions, in Toronto.

Joanne, as you will have guessed, is the daughter.

Now I'm gulping again. The intensity of the talk we had on the radio comes rushing back.

People who have listened to "Morningside" for a long time and, as they frequently say, feel they know me before they meet me in these lineups, are nevertheless sometimes stuck for words. ("But I'm cuter than you thought, aren't I?" I say to break the tension – I am, too.) Now, I know how they feel. I have shared a moment of high emotion with the lovely young person who stands at my autographing table, asked her the most intimate questions and now, face-to-face, I don't know what to say to her. Not at all. I long for the privacy of radio, with only a few hundred thousand people listening.

I blurt out that I would like her to have a copy of the book.

"But I've already bought this one," she smiles.

I explain the story to the people in the line behind her, nearly all of whom are familiar with it. Sharing Joanne's pleasure, they are happy to wait.

I sign the book I have charged on my Visa. My handwriting is even shakier than usual. On the radio, I could have turned my mike off, and kept my sloppy emotions to myself.

Suzuki and Greenspan: I didn't think they worried
David Suzuki arrives to talk about his autobiographical *Metamorphosis: Stages in a Life*, and gives me a chance – or so I think – to clear up a goof I pulled yesterday, when we taped three pieces with Eddie Greenspan, on his autobiographical *Greenspan: The Case for the*

Defence, written with the help of his friend George Jonas.

The goof came about because, as usual, I had been reading – reading *at*, in my interviewer's way – both books at once. In each case, I had found a wealth of the kind of anecdote I seek, and the endpapers of both books are filled with my scribbles. Yesterday, I chose a story from Greenspan's college days to begin part one, to send a signal of my intimate knowledge of his – or Jonas's – work and to get him spinning some tales. "Tell me," I said, "about the time when you were a student at Western and you were afraid of being charged with a crime because you had deposited a number of coins in a bank just after a robbery and . . ."

"Well, the story's true," said Greenspan, puzzled, "but I didn't go to Western."

Oops. Wrong autobiography.

Now, as we wait for the theme to end before my chat with Suzuki, I tell David how I had confused him with the lawyer.

"But *I* didn't go to Western either," he says.

Oh, dear. He went to *high school* in London, whereas Greenspan went to . . .

Ah, forget it. At least I didn't screw this one up on the air.

Greenspan, by the way, loves radio, and I sometimes think the program he and Jonas do together, "Scales of Justice", matters as much to him as his brilliant courtroom victories. He would like to sit in some day as host of "Morningside." I happen to think he'd be good at it, but Gloria disagrees. To duck the question, which he raises every time I see him, I tell him he can do my job for a morning if I can appear in court for him, defending one of his accused murderers.

"OK," he said once. I still don't know if he was kidding.

Yesterday, to my astonishment (for he appears to have an unshakable ego), Eddie was still upset by a lukewarm review of *The Case for the Defence* in the *Globe* on Saturday. "I worked hard on the book," he said, "and some guy just picked it up and attacked me."

I tell this to Suzuki, too, when we've finished our on-air chat.

"Me, too," he says.

"But you haven't *had* any bad reviews yet, David."

"No," he says. "But I'm worried."

Funny, isn't it? Two of the most accomplished and – justly –

celebrated men you could imagine, trembling over the reception of their books. The ego is a strange thing. Thank goodness I don't have any, eh?

Home . . . at Last

Harry Bruce

ere at Port Shoreham, N.S., a cold deserted bay looms in the south, and coyotes murder sheep. The closest movie house is 45 miles away, winter hatefully lingers till just before the black flies ruin spring, the shrieks of crows torture anyone who's still in bed at dawn, and Penny and I have at last found the home we've never had before and will never leave again.

After 33 years of bouncing from city to city, to yet another city, we have settled forever in a place that's about as citified as squashed porcupines on a highway. We miss the treats of urban life but not the restlessness that kept us wandering from the time Louis St. Laurent was prime minister, Wayne and Shuster were appearing on "The Ed Sullivan Show," and James Dean starred in *Rebel Without a Cause.*

We are home at last.

I don't know what caused the restlessness, but from the moment we married – I was barely 21 and Penny, 19 – we shared something with a character described by American author Elmer Kelton. We were "always fidgeting around to go, like a horse in an ant bed." Heaven knows how many million couples have felt the same itch.

I was an editorial gypsy. I joined the *Ottawa Journal* as a 20-year-old reporter in 1955, and between then and 1970, I worked for the *Ottawa Journal* twice, the *Globe and Mail* twice, and *Maclean's* twice. I also did time with *Saturday Night,* the *Toronto Star,* the *Star Weekly,* the *Canadian Magazine* and a task force on federal government information services. I quit the *Ottawa Journal* so Penny and I could live forever in England. We were back in

Ottawa within a year. I quit *The Globe* so we could live forever in California. We were back in Toronto within two months. Before moving to Nova Scotia in 1971, I'd held – and quit – 12 good jobs. In *Bluenose* country, the pattern continued.

If no job was ever quite satisfying, no dwelling was ever quite home. In 33 years, we've lived in three flats, six apartments, two cottages and six houses. We settled mostly in big cities, but also – and for no reason that made any sense – in the villages of Newcastle, Ont., and Prospect, N.S. Our three children grew up in an apartment and a house in Toronto, a cottage on Toronto Island, a house in Newcastle, a house in Ottawa, the house in Newcastle again, a house in Prospect, and a house and two apartments in Halifax. As soon as they made friends in one neighborhood, we moved to another.

To add alarm to their rootlessness, we spent weekends prowling the countryside in search of The Perfect Home. From Ottawa, we drove south to inspect brick mansions with mansard roofs that overlooked the St. Lawrence River. From Toronto, we drove north to consider this or that handyman's special on Georgian Bay. From Halifax, we scooted through the Annapolis Valley. In elegant wooden towns such as Wolfville and Annapolis Royal, we squandered the Saturday afternoons of real estate agents. We did the same thing all along the south shore of Nova Scotia. We had learned nothing from the madness that, only a few years before, had inspired us to sell our house in downtown Toronto so we could buy another one in Newcastle – 50 miles from my job at the *Toronto Star*.

But now that our children have grown up, moved back to Toronto and started their own cycles of restlessness, we have come home to the last house we'll ever own. I'm 54, Penny's 52, and we know we'll never move again. Goodbye to moving companies, rented vans, bare walls, change-of-address cards and gloomy yard sales to dump junk that's not worth taking on yet another ride down the road. Goodbye to biting our nails while waiting for someone to buy our place. Goodbye, too, to all those times we tensely debated raising our bid for what would surely turn out to be, at long last, the home of our dreams.

We're through with all that because we recently moved to a farmhouse that Richard Bruce, my great-great-grandfather, built in 1847. It's in Port Shoreham, a remote corner of Nova Scotia in which his Scottish-born father, James, had settled more than half a century earlier. I knew this house as a boy. My father sent me here from Toronto in the summer of 1946 to live with his mother and sisters, and I slept in the bedroom that had been his when the King of England was still the playful Edward VII.

I was here in later summers, too, and it now seems that, for most of my life, forces I barely understood – family history, my father's poetry and fiction, my own love of the sea – were conspiring to displease me with all other places, and to draw me eastward, ever eastward, to the one spot on earth where I'd feel totally, definitely and forever at home. Luckily for me, Penny is like the wives of earlier Port Shoreham Bruces in a crucial respect: she, too, feels right about calling this property her one and only home. There are ghosts here, she says, but they're friendly ghosts.

For my Aunt Anna, a tiny vigorous woman of 95, we tacked a small apartment on the east side of the house. But the original structure is a white, wooden, two-storey job with a peaked dormer over the front door to add space and light to the upstairs hall. The house sits below the highway, and beyond it, to the south, Chedabucto Bay stretches down to the sea and up to Guysborough town. Inside, our ceilings are so low we had to take the railing off the stairs to move a queen-size bed into our bedroom. Nineteenth-century Bruces were short both physically and financially. The four upstairs bedrooms are smaller than some people's bathrooms, and we destroyed the downstairs bedroom to enlarge the kitchen. It's the only ample room in the entire old house. It's where our wood-burning stove crackles all winter and where we sit while gazing at the sprawling bay.

The beach on Chedabucto Bay is a 15-minute walk from the farmhouse, and down there on a wooded bluff, our cottage sits by itself. It's a plain, brown, rangy affair with big windows that face the sea, a box stove that gobbles birch and balsam fir, and a floor made of tongue-and-groove boards. During storms, the cottage seems as cosy as a little ship, and infinitely safer. Even more than the ancient family history and the ancient Bruce house, it makes our 85 acres feel like home. A cousin of mine built it for us when we first moved to Nova Scotia. We kept hopping around in Prospect and Halifax, but we could always count on the cottage staying exactly as it was, exactly as we wanted it to be, with the surf whispering on the beach below and the breeze whispering in the balsam fir above.

The cottage was like a bonfire; the focus for our warmest family huddles. We have no electricity or running water down there, and now – whenever I light one of our old coal-oil lamps or bathe in the rainwater from the plastic garbage buckets under the downpipes – I remember the board games, the charades contests, the stunts with the battery-driven tape recorder, the skinny-dipping in the icy bay or the night our sailboat, *Moonshadow*, came loose from her mooring. When we awoke in the morning, she was a mile offshore, drifting toward Spain. Taking turns at the oars, our oldest son, Alec, and I rowed out to rescue her.

He was 13 at the time. Now he's a newspaper reporter in Toronto with a wife and two daughters, but he has never forgotten our voyage on that long-gone morning. When I root among the 1973 comic books in the cottage, and the romance novels, dominoes, decks of playing cards, swimming flippers, goggles, and the shells, bones and buoys that our children dragged up from the beach, I know that, now and then, all three of them still think of the place. It was where we had our best times together, and even though we were never there for more than three weeks out of every year, it came closer to being our real home than any of our year-round dwellings. For Penny and me, it was where the heart was, and now we can get there in a few minutes.

We have another sailboat, and to honor the days when we romped on Chedabucto Bay with our youngsters, we have given the new craft the old name. This past summer, we sailed in the paths of forgotten schooners built by forgotten Bruces, and the second *Moonshadow* thrilled Alec, who's now 28. Alec's wife, Vivien, was aboard one afternoon, too, and so were their daughters, Melinda, 7, and Jessica, 4. They had all come down from Toronto for a visit, just as I had done 42 years before.

I was 11 then, going on 12, and if anyone had asked me if I thought I'd ever become a grandfather, I might have replied that my chances of becoming Batman were better. Now, the little gatherings of my clan, here at Port Shoreham, are sweet confirmation that these acres, this grass, this farmhouse, this cottage, this boat, beach, bay and messy sub-Arctic jungle all add up to Home.

I feel *querencia* for this lonely land. *Querencia* is a Spanish word that means "affection for the place one calls home." *The New Yorker* once described it as "the satisfaction of a groundhog surveying his domain in the evening from his customary post outside his burrow" and "the tender serenity of the people on the porch once again noticing the groundhog on the familiar field."

Having found our home, Penny and I now reminisce about all the places that never quite filled the bill. We recall escaping the furnace-room heat of midsummer Ottawa by swimming among the log booms on the Gatineau River; a magical party that lasted till a clean Sunday dawn at our cottage on Toronto Island; sipping exquisite martinis with friends in the magazine business on the roof of Toronto's Park Plaza Hotel; the first time we saw porpoises rollicking like giddy fools off Prospect; and the day in Halifax that we went to a concert starring Luciano Pavarotti, and then, his sublime voice still ringing in our heads, walked home under trees so heavy with rain that leaves on the sagging branches soaked our hair.

We don't yearn to repeat these experiences, but we're glad we had them; and in an odd way, feeling *querencia* for this small, bleak homestead makes me feel it for the whole, huge country. I feel it not only for the places I've known so well, but also for the towns and mountains out west that I've never even seen. We're going to drive to the Pacific Ocean soon. Once more, we'll hit the road. This time, however, we will know exactly where all our trips will end. Like *Moonshadow*, we now have a permanent mooring with the right kind of chain, and next Canada Day, for the first time in my life, I shall raise the red Maple Leaf over my home.

A Village Childhood

June Callwood

Villages are carriers of the tribal wisdom. Canadians who grow up in very small, stable communities have a particular perspective of the country. For us, Canada isn't huge and impersonal; shaped as we are by the scale of a village, we always see the country as manageable, intimate, sane.

I was raised in Belle River, a tiny community in southwest Ontario with a population then of about 800 people. My family moved from Belle River when I was 10 years old. Though I have lived ever since in cities (Kitchener, Regina, Brantford and, for 45 years, Toronto) I am still a villager. The experience of being raised in Belle River clings to me; villages are the central metaphor of my life. My theology, a homemade one, has much to do with my observation of how villages work.

The primary lesson of growing up in small villages is safety. When I read the seminal studies of John Bowlby and René Spitz about the searing consequences of emotional deprivation in infancy, I came to appreciate what I had always known: the courage to grow comes from being treasured early in life. People can't be open to change and trusting of others unless they have internalized a secure environment.

In my mind's eye, Toronto is not a huge metropolis but a composition of dozens of small, personal villages, which I cosily inhabit concurrently. In the sense I mean it, everyone lives in villages. For each, there is one village made up of people regularly seen in the workplace, and another village drawn from the neighborhood in which one lives, and another village of friends who come together socially, and a village of former schoolmates now scattered but readily reconstituted into a clan with a single encounter, and another village, very small and the one closest to the heart, which is populated by the people one loves.

The great novelist Margaret Laurence used a different word for village. At almost every annual meeting of The Writers' Union of Canada she ever attended, there would be a point when she would rise anxiously, her voice shaking with the intensity of her feelings, to try to restore the sense of camaraderie that had slipped away during a wrangle about fees or the Canada Council or whatever.

"We writers are a *tribe*," she'd cry. Exactly.

Writers are a tribe, a village, and so are computer hacks, and Blue Jay fans, and people who have had openheart surgery, and chess players, and mothers of newborns, and people thrown together in a disaster. A common experience, whatever it is, enables people to make bridges to one another across chasm-wide disparities of age, personality and background. What they share is a strong force that outweighs their differences; they cannot entirely be strangers. They live in a certain terrain, which they can discuss without having to explain it.

When people match experience, they are kin. Even motorists caught in a traffic jam will catch one another's eye and, for that moment of mutual frustration, exasperation and resignation, will have a bond.

"What do you do?" strangers inquire when they are thrown together. Or, "Are you from the West?" Even, "Cold, isn't it?" will suffice. They are really saying, "Where's our village? Unless we find it, this relationship isn't going anywhere."

A shared moment dissolves isolation. Strangers become a cohesive group when it rains on a picnic ground. In a room almost full of men, the few women present will exchange a look that has layers of meaning only to them. Parents whose children have died do not need words to convey understanding when they meet.

An African, asked what he remembered about being raised in a village, replied eloquently, "Many hands." My version of that sense of being cradled is "many eyes." I could wander everywhere in Belle River without being out of sight of some adult who knew who I was and where I was supposed to be at that hour. If I fell, the nearest adult picked me up and gave comfort. I went into my Uncle Mike Lavoie's butcher shop, fascinated by the wood shavings and the chopping block; crossed the street to my father's ramshackle tinning plant down by the bridge and said hello to my parents, both of them sweating over a vat of melted metal where they repaired the milk cans of dairy farmers; continued down the dirt road by the river to see my greatgrandparents, Mimi and Pipi Sauve, tiny people who always had cookies; and back to stand beside my Grandfather Bill Lavoie in his deserted restaurant where customers never came in those darkest years of the Depression. I leaned against his wheelchair, at peace with his silence, contentedly watching that dark, handsome man playing solitaire endlessly with a ragged deck of cards.

Nanny Garber was a vivacious little girl of about my age. Her parents owned a dress shop near my grandfather's stone house and her affectionate family lived in the back of it. The village treated the Garbers with coolness. A flat look came into the eyes of adults when I said I was going to Nanny's. I suppose it was because the Garbers were the only Jewish people in Belle River, but at the time I was baffled that anyone would disapprove of them. However, it didn't matter. The Roman Catholic majority in Belle River didn't entirely accept me either because my father was Protestant, so Nanny and I imagined ourselves outcasts; it was the delicious basis of our friendship.

I felt the same tone of reservation in Tilbury, a village a few miles west of Belle River, where my grandparents Harold and Margaret Callwood lived. They were pillars of the Church of England, and I somehow knew that their friends had reservations about me because my mother was a Roman Catholic. Grandfather Callwood was a genial, much admired man, a county judge, who unfailingly had time for me, and my grandmother was the sweetest, kindest, most forgiving woman I have ever known. I adored seeing her dressed splendidly in a long white gown with a wide red ribbon across her ample bosom, an outfit she wore for events involving her membership in something called the Eastern Star. When her friends came on summer afternoons to play euchre, examining me with birdlike curiosity for signs of wanton popery, I proudly served them plates of small cakes toppling with icing that I had helped her make on a kitchen table covered with flowered oilcloth.

My other pal in Belle River was my grandfather's Chinese cook, a small, bent man who often placed two chairs on the sidewalk in front of the restaurant so we could watch the passing cars and farmers' wagons. As we whiled away the time, he tried to teach me to say my name in Chinese. I think at one time I could, and some other words as well.

I was the only one in Belle River who knew that he cried. He would weep in the tiny bedroom off the restaurant kitchen, sitting on his cot bent over cracked snapshots of Chinese children and a Chinese woman. I had nothing to say against the vastness of his despair, but he liked to have me with him while he cried. I waited without anxiety, watching him, neither of us embarrassed, until he finished. Then he would wipe his face and fix me something to eat.

I was a privileged child because of Belle River. There I swam free in a cocoon of protection. Generations of my family surrounded me with affection and approval. My childhood was drenched in continuity, freedom and safety. In winter twilight, I could find my way home without trepidation after piano lessons at the convent, or on summer nights climb the cherry tree behind our house and look at the stars. In August, I went to the tomato cannery where wagons waited in a long line in front of the weighing scale. Farmers would let me sit beside them on the high wagon seat where I could watch patient horses switching flies off their wide rears with their tails and eat sun-warm tomatoes, the most delicious taste in the world. I went to school flanked by a swarm of cousins.

I also learned from Nanny Garber and my own small brushes with bigotry about injustice. The Chinese cook taught me more – that when the system is not fair, real people suffer real pain.

Since then, I see the village model as the best. When a friend of mine, Margaret Frazer, was diagnosed with terminal cancer, I assumed that it would be possible to find enough people to ensure her support for her wish to die at home. Some 60 people rallied to help in shifts around the clock for three months. They came from two of her villages – one group from the congregation of Holy Trinity Anglican Church, and the other from the network of people centred on Nellie's Hostel for Women where Margaret was a dedicated volunteer.

Some of us could cook; some could sew; some could repair a garden trellis or tend the compost; some could sing. The "Margaret team," as we still think of ourselves, became a village. Our reunions on the anniversary of Margaret's death are joyful. For a brief time, we were the human tribe functioning at its best. We emerged enriched and intensely grateful.

About 10 years ago, I used to meet with a group of people in the basement of Nellie's to discuss an emerging crisis in social services. All over North America, teenagers suddenly were deciding to keep their babies and raise them instead of placing them for adoption. For the most part, these teenage mothers had little family support. They were school dropouts, unskilled and unsure of themselves.

The solution was to build a village we called Jessie's. It's a centre that provides in one place almost all the resources a teenage mother would find in a caring village: hospitality, a meal, used baby clothes, a nurse to consult, a doctor who comes by, the loan of a crib and stroller, a schoolteacher who is kind, a place for the baby to play, people to ask about parenting problems, affection, approval, support.

In social work literature, Jessie's is admiringly called "a multi-service agency." Its multiservice approach – combining health, counselling, education and what information is available on low-income housing – is seen as the wave of the future. To me, it's just Belle River moved to Bathurst Street in Toronto. It simply makes sense to put helpful components together in one place, as a village does.

Wild roses grew in our backyard in Belle River. I looked for them when I went back two years ago, but they were gone. However, Belle River is still there. Belle River is everywhere.

A Different Kind of Country

Michele Landsberg

I spent last July 4 high up in the Empire State Building. Far below, Manhattan lay dazzled in Sunday sunshine. From the windows of the CBC's offices (I had come to the studio to do a "Cross-Country Checkup" program on U.S.-Canadian differences), you could see the whole city lying quiet in the silvery embrace of two rivers, the Statue of Liberty facing out to sea with its gigantic welcome, and the tantalizing jumble of towers, spires, tenements, mansions, hidden rooftop nooks and gardens.

For the next two hours in the windowless little studio, I listened to voices crackling in from the farthest reaches of my native land. And I might as well admit that at the beginning of the show, having wrenched myself away from the glorious view, I was acutely aware of my own ambivalence about my imminent departure for home.

"Don't you miss Canada?" visitors from home would often ask with a kind of smug anticipation. "Don't you miss all the trees?" I would look at them in baffled silence. When you are living for a while in one of the world's most intense, vibrant, crowded, contradictory, infuriating and fascinating cities, you do not pine for the sight of a maple.

In fact, I fit better in New York, where my impulsive, outspoken, critical character, my gregariousness (I talk to strangers on elevators) and my quickness to embrace new friends made me feel instantly at home. I didn't miss trees. But what I did miss was a web of values, assumptions and political choices that mark us as unique in the world, but that nobody ever seems to mention when we Canadians settle down to our favorite parlor game of defining the national identity. So I wasn't looking forward to the radio program, whose advance billing was "a celebration of our differences." I was afraid those trees would come up again, metaphorically speaking. And they did. But, to my surprise and pleasure, even more callers spoke of the things that I believe truly make Canada different.

In the United States, it's winner take all and the loser be damned. American popular culture idolizes wealth and celebrity, no matter how venally they've been gained; social policy punishes the poor because they're really believed to be the authors of their own misfortunes. Canada, as the callers repeatedly stressed, has a different ethos. Public medical insurance, public hospitals and universities, paid maternity leave and government support for the arts are all aspects of our commitment to collective responsibility.

After listening for two hours to those voices, I ended by reminding myself why there was no real choice: I love New York; I have been happy there, but I could never live there permanently. Because I would have no one to vote for.

The act of voting expresses my deepest allegiance, my sense of who I am and what I wish for myself and the world. I know that for many Canadians, the vote is a sometime thing, a matter of no great importance. Some (and this staggers me) don't even bother to vote. But to me, Canada's political structure is its finest aspect, our political choices are our most praiseworthy achievement. They're what bind me to this country, what make me proud when I'm away and what make me feel it's worth it to come home.

Does that seem preposterous? In the fever of the free trade debate, all three parties paid homage to what makes us distinctive as a country. All three singled out unemployment insurance and medicare, both pioneered by the democratic left. The left has also influenced institutions such as the National Film Board (NFB) and the CBC, which have set nationally accepted standards for independence and excellence in film and broadcasting. Once, I proudly showed some NFB documentaries to a sophisticated crowd of New Yorkers: for all their cultural riches, they were agog that women filmmakers in Canada could actually produce serious documentaries about peace, the environment and the Nairobi Women's Conference all with public funding. "You say the *government* funds these films?" they asked me with amazement.

Americans are awestruck when they hear some of our intelligent and balanced news shows, such as "Sunday Morning" or "As It

Happens." And they marvel over the quality of our children's entertainment: Raffi and Sharon, Lois and Bram, the Vancouver Children's Festival and CBC's "Anne of Green Gables." I always explain to them that our standards for children's entertainment are higher because they were established by noncommercial broadcasting. If we Canadians are more critical of and less susceptible to the crassest forms of commercial culture, we can thank those who inspired the founding of the Film Board and the CBC.

And then there is Canada's system of universal health care. I have a particularly personal reason for my commitment to public medical insurance. When I was pregnant with my second child, my parents went off to New York to attend a family wedding. It was winter; my father, a burly, strong 72-year-old who had just been pronounced totally fit by his doctor, shovelled the snow from the driveway so they could drive to the airport. A day later, in New York, he suffered a massive heart attack.

Hospitals in New York, in 1967, cost a minimum of $90 a day, an astronomic sum by my family's standards. So my father stayed in bed at my aunt and uncle's house. And a week later, when he got out of bed to go to the bathroom, his heart stopped forever. If he had been at home in Toronto, where medical care was not limited to those who can afford it, he might have lived to see his grandson who was born four months later; he might have lived for years.

Medicare, to me, is not abstract. It is life and death; it is a national agreement that the almighty dollar is not the ultimate arbiter of human worth.

I grew up Jewish, a certified outsider in this country. I shared in all the freedom and security that Canada had to offer. But in a hundred subtle ways, all of them painfully clear to a sensitive child, I was made to know that I was marginal. Not entitled. Not quite Canadian.

The first time I felt as though I belonged to larger Canadian society was the day I marked my first ballot. I was 21 and so overcome by excitement and pride that my hands shook, and when I left the polling booth, I was so rattled by emotion that I suddenly couldn't be sure I had made my mark in the right square.

My parents were not political. I remember that my father voted Conservative in the Diefenbaker sweep, and that at other times, I heard the name CCF. But these were background murmurs. It was only at university that it dawned on me there was a remedy –

political action – for the injustices, particularly the injustices to women and minorities, that I saw around me. The year I graduated, I volunteered as an NDP canvasser in my own riding. We lost, but the effort was exhilarating. There was another federal election the following year; I volunteered again, met the new campaign manager and married him six weeks later.

I was 24 years old when my husband, Stephen Lewis, was elected to the Ontario Legislature a few months after our wedding. Our riding organization held a triumphant meeting right after the victory and invited me to become the president of the women's auxiliary. I looked around the packed meeting hall, filled with dynamic, hardworking women who had virtually run the campaign, not to mention keeping the organization alive during all the years before victory was ours. With the presumption of youth and inexperience, I stood up, thanked them for the honor, and suggested that the auxiliary be abolished. After all, women were the backbone of the party and not auxiliary in any sense of the word. It's a measure of my party's early and steadfast commitment to women's equality that my cheeky proposal was instantly applauded and adopted. Where else could a budding Canadian feminist, in those pre-women's movement days, have found such instinctive allies? Day care and equal pay were party platforms long before the public warmed to those ideas. And it was an NDP member of Parliament, Margaret Mitchell, who first rose in the House of Commons to speak about domestic violence (and who was greeted by raucous laughter and coarse jokes from men of the old-line parties).

In the 25 years since Stephen was first elected, politics has been our meat and potatoes, the warp and woof of our daily life, the lens through which we view the world. We date the events of our married life by elections and byelections; we refer to our previous homes by the names of the ridings they were in. And through victories and defeats and all the roller-coaster swoops and plunges of democratic politics – the moments of bitterness or cynicism, the years of arduous effort – I've never doubted that having a socialist option in Canada is one of our country's true glories. Every time I cast my vote, I affirm not only my personal political choice but my sense of being happily Canadian, of really belonging here.

In a small way, I share with my political colleagues in all the strengths and benefits we have contributed to the Canadian way of life. As a journalist, I've fought for women's equality and for a whole range of health and children's issues, from treatment for the emotionally disturbed to enriched opportunities in public schools. I haven't felt alone because my party, too, was fighting for the same goals. And I am grateful to my country for its political broadmindedness.

An old adage has it that you can't legislate human nature. The idea is that it's no use trying to fight prejudice or selfishness or cruelty to children by passing laws against them. Precisely the opposite is true. When a law clearly states that bigotry or violence is illegal and will be punished, eventually the social consensus shapes itself around that perception. Over the generations, Canadians have come to believe, among other things, that decent basic medical care is a human right, and that hospitals should not be making profits out of human misery. We have come to believe that the airwaves belong to everyone, not just to the moneymakers; that society owes support and encouragement to the new mother to enable her to nurture her baby. We believe that artistic expression is not just some private quirk but an essential way in which we Canadians can come to know and define ourselves, and is therefore worth our collective support. We hold to the idea that natural self-interest must be tempered by consideration for the common good.

These assumptions, not some milky, vague "niceness," are the fibre of the Canadian national character. They are deeply different from the assumptions that underlie American society. We should recognize, celebrate and safeguard them; they are as Canadian as maple leaves, sparkling rivers and butter tarts. As lovable and maybe, as perishable.

Another Kind of Place

Roy MacGregor

The first time I saw it, I thought it was the ugliest place on earth. A northern exposure. Too damp. Too steep. Overgrown. No rocks to dive off; no sand to walk on. The waterline beginning the instant the hemlock gave up.

I had come to this ugly patch of Muskoka Highland because, back then, I would do anything to be with a certain young woman. Even if it meant mosquitoes and raspberry-cane scratches and tromping around on slippery moss behind a man, her father, who saw a dock where I could see only deadheads, a cedar deck where I could see only poplar scrub and toadstools.

His $800 had been the only offer on this sloping pie-shaped government lot on Camp Lake. That should have told him something. But so determined was this quiet high school teacher to have his own sacred spot on the water that he probably would have bid against himself to win it. For him, it was a lifelong dream come true. Here he would build his fires. Here he would work with his hands. Here he would fall asleep to the soft kiss of surfacing trout, awake to the alarm of the loon. For me, it was nothing of the sort. I was, but did not know it then, a cottage snob.

I had come from a strangely privileged background, one that had everything to do with circumstance and nothing whatsoever to do with money. I knew no one else from my baby boom generation who had been toilet-trained on an outdoor privy and who could remember being taught how to turn a tap and flip a light switch after we moved from the bush into town. My father was a lumberman who worked in Ontario's magnificent and wild Algonquin Park. My grandfather had been chief ranger. For me, the park could not only never be replaced, it must never be challenged.

How could anything ever compare? The old ranger's reward for blazing the trail that would one day become Highway 60 through the park had been permission to select the lot of his choice on which to build the place he would live. He went to the heart of his beloved park, Lake of Two Rivers, and chose a long, high point facing south where the morning sun would walk up gently slanting rocks on the east side and the evening sun would pour its rich, thick light over high, dramatic rocks to the west.

He built a magnificent two-storey log home on the highest point; built it and a beautiful granite-and-quartz fireplace and three outer cabins and an icehouse with his own hands and wrote the date and signed his name on the last piece of trim he set on Sept. 10, 1940.

It seemed he had created this Eden for the dozens of grand-children who swarmed over the point each summer, a few of whom were lucky enough to live there each year from the moment school in the town let out until it let back in. My older brother and I built a baseball diamond around the woodpiles. My sister and I built an entire miniature world on a sheltered bay by the point, with small roads and stone steps and small graveyards for minnows and tadpoles and newts and crayfish where, if you had any decency about you, you spoke low and stepped carefully.

It was a world of coal oil lamps, huge ice blocks packed in sawdust, fresh trout, Archie comics and deer that ate from your hand. You awoke to the slam of a screen door, fell asleep to the howl of the timber wolves on the far side of the lake.

And this – this pitiful, overgrown, ugly hill on the side of a lake that couldn't be bothered forming a proper shore – *this* was supposed to compete with such a memory?

The '60s twisted into the '70s. A bulldozer came in and rammed a rough road into the lake that had no shore. The teacher retired and he and his wife began to construct their outrageous dream, while I shook my head in dismay. They laid footings and hauled lumber and, eventually, a small cottage went up. He built his deck. He dug a hole on the only space that wasn't rock and put up an outhouse. He built a crib in winter and a dock over the sunken crib in the summer. Furniture came from old relatives and from an insatiable urge to scavenge back road dumps. Water would still be carried up from the lake, but there would be electricity.

Gradually, the hill took on a new personality, but it could never compete with the old ranger's log cottage on Lake of Two Rivers. It did not matter that the real cottage was no longer there (the ranger had died, an American had bought the place and, eventually, they tore it down in a fit of returning the park to its original state) for the footings and chinking and cribs of Lake of Two Rivers were still solid and lasting in my mind.

A hundred Teen Town dances later and the certain young woman and I were no longer teenagers but married. Too soon, it seemed, we had four children. Much too soon, the retired teacher died and, naturally, we were expected to step in and help his wife become to the cottage what he had been: keeper, handyman, curator, lover. The real question, of course, was whether or not this pitiful little attempt at a cottage could ever step in and become to me what the old ranger's cottage had been. A selfish thought, but I did not know then that a cottage is a state of mind, not a fixed address.

The cottage is an idea that snuggles up against the soul of Canadians the way Brighton does to Britons and possum-hunting does to Alabamians. It is who we are, our statement on the bush and the north and the seasons. It is the way we homestead on summer, as if it might be somehow possible to build a better life away from the April muck and November sleet and January hopelessness. It is the way we shake off our cluttered city lives and are permitted to pioneer momentarily away from the madness and stress. It is where we would live, if only we could figure out how.

It matters not whether it's called a cottage or a camp, whether owned or rented or, best of all, borrowed; it matters not whether we speak of $700,000 solar-heated three-car-garage glass inventions on the shores of Georgian Bay or a tent struck on the shores of the Qu'Appelle River. A true cottage finds you, not the other way around.

And that's just what happened with this rustic little cottage on the sloping side of the lake with no shore. Slowly the place crept up on me. It took years, but that, I suppose, is the great curiosity of rituals that matter: when they first come along, we fail to recognize them for what they are. But then, one day, after a decade or more of working up to it, you find yourself breathing deeply when the door bursts open on a cold and musty cottage. Someone always says the bugs are either better or worse than last year. They are never the same. You walk to the raspberry patches and lay grand plans for pies, knowing that, in fact, no raspberry will ever make it out in any container other than a child's stomach. The kids check in the bay for the sunken boat that has been there for 20 years. They look under the dock for the snapping turtle that collects a thousand missed heartbeats a year.

I tried to explain to these children why my cottage was so much more special. I would tell them how the old ranger they never knew would stand at the dock and watch us swim on our own the distance between the boardwalk and booms, and how it was worth a dollar to anyone who could. If you could swim this distance, the reward was also to swim beyond the boom, and if you could swim from the boom to a distant rock, you were qualified then to begin diving off the high rocks to the west.

My own children demanded a dollar when they, too, could swim between the pier dock their grandfather had built and the small floating dock their mother built, then two dollars if they could swim from there to the diving platform of the next cottage down. This done, they decided it qualified them to try to swim across the bay. It was only when I realized that some of them might someday be measuring their own children in such a manner – telling them, God forbid, about an old eccentric they never knew – that I realized it is not the place but the experience we hand down.

Their grandparents' tiny cottage on the side of a hill – northern exposure, no shoreline – has been twisting as deep into their own souls as the old ranger's place had in mine. And if it is the experience that is important, not the place, then it suddenly no longer mattered so much that someone had come and bought the ranger's place away from us and torn it down, taken it away and burned what was left. The experience no one could touch, not with bulldozers, not with fire, certainly not with money.

I had to learn to see this other place through the eyes of my own children. Long into summer nights, I have stood along this harsh shoreline with each of them, three girls and a boy, as each child passed through that remarkable phase that comes only to five-year-olds, when they stand, shaking and shivering, one bare foot scratching the bites on the other calf, their hands around a fishing rod while bats swoop out of the high spruce. Sometimes we hear radios playing all the way from the far island. Sometimes we hear the trout jumping as they feed. Sometimes it seems as if the stars hang from the trees and are thicker than the mosquitoes. Sometimes a child even catches something.

The Canadian summer is a transitory joy, one so fleeting that even its difficulties are treasured. It is our secret time, the two or three or, with luck, four weeks when we believe we are our truest selves. It is our sweetest thought, one held in parentheses by the *opening up* and the *closing up*, the season beginning with sparklers and ending in embers, when suddenly, without warning, the seasons reverse. The leaves no longer shade but reveal; relief now is to be found inside rather than out, in fire rather than water. On an October morning so cold that the black lake steams, an outdoor toilet loses its July charm.

This is when we take summer down to the small shed and put her away with a half tank of mixed gasoline, a single flipper and three reels that somebody with half a brain should be able to fix. This is when the air comes out of the cottage, when you pull the small plastic plugs with your teeth and stand stomping inner tubes and plastic boats while your own stale breath from early July hisses back at you.

It has only been in the last year that I have come to understand that the cottage – any cottage – is where children who are lucky enough to get to one keep their summers. If summers are the jewels of their little lives, then the cottage is the velvet box where summer is stored.

This I learned in the dead of summer, at the end of one of those heavy, hot weeks when the days seem to follow each other with the loyalty and rhythm of parading elephants. My oldest daughter, Kerry, now 13, was sitting down by the water in what has, over the years, been reconstructed into her own private cottage-within-the-cottage.

There she had hauled in sand to make a beach that mostly washed away. She had strung a rope from a branch for swinging out over the water and letting go with a scream. She had built a dock that wobbled. She had put in her own benches and, using spruce boughs, built her own beach umbrella for shade. The branches had turned brown as rust and the needles were falling off, but she sat below it with a comic on her lap staring out over the water.

"Don't ever sell this place," she said. "I want my children to come here."

Sell it? We don't even own it. But none of this would mean anything to her. The place owns her.

That lesson repeated itself over Christmas. We were home in Ottawa, typical plugged-in suburbanites on a cold December evening, and the power went off. One moment all was completely normal – television roaring, ghetto blasters pounding, Christmas lights blinking – and the next moment it was not normal at all. It was totally black, completely silent. No one said a word until a match could be located and struck, producing a nearly forgotten light, pale and yellow, that sent shadows leaping against the kitchen wall.

"Neat!" someone said.

A flashlight was found and, with the flashlight, two ornamental coal oil lamps were brought from another room and lighted. The suburban kitchen filled with a liquid yellow color it had never before known. The children stared at each other and their surroundings as if they were suddenly guests in a magic house.

"It's like being at the cottage," one of them noticed.

It was not just the light, but the silence – as if for once in this bedroom community two-storey, you might hear a squirrel scamper across the roof rather than the burst of a laugh track from the television room. The two youngest children ran with the flashlight for their comforters, brought them down, wrapped themselves up with exaggerated squirms of delight and asked for a fire.

While the fire stuttered and snapped, they filled the space usually taken by television and cassette tapes by talking about their most treasured moment of the year just past.

"Remember the snapping turtle?" someone said.

"Remember the deer tracks by the sand pit?" someone answered.

I went and stood by the window, remembering another house in the bush when these same lamps would cast just enough light for an old ranger to work on his crossword puzzles and an old woman to prepare her Christmas baking. My mother would be testing the wood stove oven with the back of her hand. My father would be due soon from the mill. A brother would be reading comic books; a sister would have a jigsaw puzzle out that had been put together and taken apart so often, certain pieces looked like splayed books.

Once, as adults, my sister and I had gone back in search of our special place by the point. It was stunningly overgrown, and though we did find one spot where it looked as if stone steps had once been laid out, it was now like a Mayan ruin. The point could not live up to the memory, but the memory had not been harmed in the least by this realization. If anything, it was all the more valuable because now, it was all we would ever have of those times.

These children in their comforters by the fire were talking, I realized, of the most beautiful place I now know on earth. It is their perfect childhood memory still being formed.

"Remember the big toad?" a small voice wondered.

But before anyone could, the power surged back on. Lights, television, tapes, buzzers, clocks .

"Boooooo!" the children shouted.

It was a false alarm. The power failed; the coal oil lamps regained their place; the children cheered. And while they returned to their cottage memories, their mother and I quietly left the room to the crackling fire and their low, excited voices.

And we walked about the suburban house turning off every electrical switch we could find.

A Walk on the Wild Side

Alice Munro

Where I grew up, on the rural west side of the town of Wingham in southern Ontario, the Maitland River was at the foot of our property. The river flats and the bottomlands were generally too stony for crops, but made good pasture. There were scattered trees where the cattle could shelter from the sun, and the river provided drinking water. From the rough natural vegetation of the bottomlands and river flats, the grazing cattle produced a grassy parkland that reached to the foot of our property in a grove of elm trees within sight of the house.

Downstream to the west, and visible from our place, a wide curve of the river had broadened the flats, and to the north, it had undercut a high steep bank covered with trees – the whole being, in effect, a great amphitheatre half a mile or more in width, floored with elm and maple parkland. On the high, distant skyline back from the amphitheatre was Roly Grain's farmstead – house, barn and silo. To the south, where Roly Grain's side road joined Highway 86 just at the bridge where the river completes its curve, the village of Zetland once thrived – remembered by my father, but in my time utterly vanished. When I was young, the skyline with Roly Grain's farmstead seemed to me the end of the world, and the vanished village whose time had ended somehow filled out that idea.

This scene – an amphitheatre floored with parkland and reaching to the end of the world and joined to us by the river – was my first access to the countryside of southern Ontario, which was and has remained magical. When I was very young, I dreamt I saw a pure white horse with a jewelled bridle come down to drink at the river but I didn't think that was a dream. When I lived in British Columbia, I longed for the sight of Ontario landscape – the big solitary oaks and beeches and maples looming in a summer haze in the open fields, the carpet of leeks and trilliums and bloodroot in the sunny woods before the leaves come out, the unexpected little rough hills with their hawthorns and tough daisies, the creeks and bogs and the long smooth grassy slopes. On a motor trip home via the state of Washington, we came out of the splendid mountains and forest onto the great rolling country of the Palouse-Big Bend wheatlands, and I felt as if I had retrieved a lost part of myself, because it was something "like home."

Some 15 or so years ago, I returned to Ontario to live, not to the place where I grew up but to a small town nearby and to essentially the same landscape. But things have changed. The elm trees are gone – the last one on our flats, a seeming survivor of the Dutch elm disease, fell in a storm in 1977. The bottomlands are no longer pastured, for reasons I have not investigated, and have grown up in coarse vegetation – tall grasses, stinging nettle, joe-pye weed, wild parsnip, thistles, goldenrod, hawthorn and scrub willow, to name only a part of it – and the walkable land is gone. The local rivers and streams are not poisonously polluted but are often choked with various kinds of algae and water plants overstimulated by fertilizer runoff from cultivated fields. Even if I were to hack my way through the jungle of vegetation, the river doesn't have the swimmable water I once knew.

The amphitheatre in the curve of the river belonged to our neighbors, but I regarded it as mine, or ours, or not anyone's – accessible to everyone not afraid of cows. This was generally the rule – you could walk the countryside on private property without fear of being hauled up for trespass. Now, more and more rural land is posted against trespass, and when I walk in the country, I would seldom think of cutting across a piece of private land, posted or unposted, unless I had the owner's permission. The countryside of southern Ontario was once an unofficial recreation area for local people. For a variety of reasons – too many people, larger cultivated fields, the unpastured bottomlands – that day is gone. There has been no adequate replacement.

Two years ago my husband and I discovered the walking and bicycling trails in Wisconsin that have been converted from abandoned railways. Near Blue Mounds, a little west of Madison, on a fine summer morning, we came upon the Military Road Trail. When we are travelling, we find that our staying power is improved if we get about an hour's walk a day, and the trail was exactly what we were looking for. We walked from Blue Mounds to Barneveld, had lunch there in a pub right beside the trail, and walked back to Blue Mounds. We were so elated by this walk that we decided to change the itinerary of our trip to visit the other Wisconsin trails, and we were not disappointed. We talked about the reasons for our exhilaration and came up with something like this: "One of life's great pleasures is to feel possessive of your homeland, and one way to get that feeling is to see the country as a landscape that belongs to you and to which you belong, and to see it close up and at not too great a speed."

But Wisconsin is not our homeland. It was good to know that there was a government there that had taken this trouble to provide for its people – to recognize that the need to walk is as important as the need to drive on a highway. But it wasn't our government. So we came home with the hope that this sort of program could be started in southern Ontario, where at this very time so many railways are being abandoned. Recently one Sunday, we toured along the abandoned sections of the CPR from Credit Forks to Wingham, which has a branch to Fergus. Near Credit Forks, where the line crosses a secondary highway, we found 12 cars parked. They belonged to people who were walking the line, having clambered over the ridge of earth the company has bulldozed up to block passage to vehicles. At another crossing, we saw cyclists throwing their bikes over the barrier. All along the line from Wingham to Credit Forks, we encountered people walking and cycling, including a farmer who owned adjoining land. He said he would like to see the abandoned line become a trail. When you see valiant cyclists pumping along the thin edge of paved highways with the traffic roaring by, you can appreciate the appeal a controlled trail has for them, and you can also appreciate that the Ontario government, despite its advocacy of outdoor exercise, is doing nothing to facilitate cycling as an activity that large numbers of people could enjoy.

If the line west out of Credit Forks follows the same history as other abandoned railway lines in Ontario, there will be a brief period during which people will walk and bike along it, and then the adjoining landowners will close it down, whether by legal purchase or not. One fence across the line effectively closes the whole section between road crossings. All across the province, bits and pieces of abandoned lines can be found, fragmented by closure by adjoining landowners. These potential trails are being lost. And they are not just trails but existing corridors of vegetation. Along the Guelph to Goderich line, we saw banks of wild strawberries, thimbleberry and wild raspberry bushes, tame cherry trees and lilac bushes gone wild, and many, many young elm trees – enough, perhaps, to form a reservoir within which an immunity could be developed to the Dutch elm disease. Wouldn't it be worth preserving our vegetation, our nurseries of elm trees? (And trees growing up along the tracks would provide privacy for the landowners.)

I've turned my celebration of southern Ontario countryside into a plea, because I really believe that access to the land is a right and a necessity, just as paved roads and schools and hospitals are. I believe that it's important to our well-being. I think that people who see the landscape in this way will give thought to protecting and preserving it. The railways have been heavily subsidized, so surely we all have some claim on the lines when they are abandoned. If the provincial government would just accept custody of these lines, it would make possible a period in which interested parties could lobby for various plans, and the corridors wouldn't be immediately fragmented and lost. I hope they won't be.

What's so Hockey about Canada?

Hartley Steward

Last summer, in Ottawa, I played in a foursome at a charity golf tournament with the great Bobby Hull, the former Chicago Black Hawk around whom, 18 years ago, the World Hockey Association – a whole hockey league – was built.

On the first tee, he took a few practice swings, to the oohs and aahs of the gallery. The famous muscles still ripple and the wide, sloping shoulders that so many good hockey players have are still wide and sloping.

The golf swing is smooth and powerful, executed with the tempo and grace with which only the truly athletic are blessed. Frank Mahovlich swings like that. So does Yvan Cournoyer. Hull's drive was wonderful. Long and straight, with an afterburner that kicked in about 90 metres out.

I wasn't the only one there recalling that in the days he dominated the National Hockey League and then the WHA, Hull had far and away the hardest slap shot in professional hockey– clocked at 187 kilometres an hour. A terrifying blast of remarkable accuracy. Remember how he used to drift in over the blue line, skates wide apart, butt almost touching the ice, drifting to a good angle, letting it fly with that big, roundhouse swing of his controversial curved stick? Youngsters from Prince George, B.C., to Halifax got frostbite night after night trying to copy it.

In the big arenas, we'd be on our feet the minute he released it, cheering even if he didn't score. If he missed the net, the puck would boom off the boards, like to shake the rafters. One time, Gump Worsley, in the nets for the Montreal Canadiens, just simply skated out of the way and watched from the side of the net as the puck swooshed by. Nobody blamed him.

A lot of us remembered that as we watched Hull's drive find the middle of the fairway, somewhere down there near the first green. I turned to one of our foursome and noted, unnecessarily, that Bobby had a pretty good golf swing.

"Whaddaya think?" he said. "He's Bobby Hull, for heaven's sake."

Exactly.

In Canada, hockey players are different from you and me. But why do those who excel at this amazing sport have a special status in our country? Why is hockey not a sport like any other sport?

For Canadians, hockey has become a large part of the way we define ourselves. Even the least nationalistic of us are likely to think of hockey when we think of ourselves as a people. More than maple syrup, beavers, duck hunting, tundra or even Mel Hurtig, hockey is essentially Canadian.

And for young boys, the Blue Jays and the Expos notwithstanding, the dream, the real deep-down-in-the-young-heart dream, is still to grow up and play professional hockey, to make it to the NHL. And so their heroes are Wayne Gretzky and Mario Lemieux. For another generation they were Rocket Richard and Gordie Howe. And for yet another they were Syl Apps and Turk Broda. Because they are or were the best in the world. Isn't it wonderful that a country our size has heroes who can do this thing better than anyone else in the world?

Where I grew up, in a little town in Northern Ontario called Schumacher, hockey was a way out of the mines. On the Prairies, hundreds of youngsters, skating till their legs were numb on frozen ponds, saw a way off the farm.

Everywhere in Canada, then and now, you can see hockey rinks cleared on riverbeds and lakefronts. By winter's end, the snowbanks around them are four storeys high. Why do these kids flood their backyards in the dark of night after their homework is done and scrape away the new-fallen snow at six in the morning in the biting cold? So they can be heroes in their hometown, of course. And maybe someday heroes in their country. And that means being a hockey player.

When I was just getting into my teens, Frank Mahovlich lived down the street from us. He was only a few years older than me, but even then we knew he had something special. A lot of my friends might make the big league some day, but we had no doubt about Frank. Nor, of course, did Frank.

We watched, with as much pride as his parents, as he skated with that long, easy stride through midget, juvenile and then St. Mike's and finally to the Toronto Maple Leafs. Those of us who weren't going to make it knew we'd still be able to say we grew up with Frank Mahovlich.

Schumacher wasn't much different from most towns where winter came in October and stayed seven months. The biggest building in town was the McIntrye Arena, a shrine to hockey, shared grudgingly with figure skaters and wrestling matches. For us young men, it was the centre of our lives.

The fact is, that even if you were never going to be a Frank Mahovlich, you had to play hockey in towns like Schumacher. Hockey was what it was all about. From hockey flowed all the good things in a young man's life. Friends, status, adulation, rewards of all kinds, including maybe someday money and fame. For a young boy not to play hockey in Schumacher was pretty near unthinkable. And besides, all the girls worth dating were sitting in the red seats at the arena every game.

So that's where we had to be.

We would make our predawn pilgrimage there morning after morning through the cold and snow, without a complaint, lugging our duffel bags jammed with skates and mildewed pads and jocks, to practise an hour before school.

There was no place a young boy would rather be. Even I, who knew from the beginning I would never be a good player, couldn't get enough of it. We loved the cold, clean smell of it, the steam rising off the newly flooded ice, even the grate of the scrapers as we trudged in a line around the rink. Even empty, it was comfortable. It was where the hockey was.

The domination of our lives by hockey didn't end there.

At 9:05 every Saturday night, we'd be home in front of the radio for "Hockey Night in Canada": "Good evening, hockey fans in Canada and the United States. This is Foster Hewitt coming to you from the gondola at Maple Leaf Gardens." If the Leafs were winning, as they mostly did in those days, it would be a perfect night.

There were only six teams in the league then, so we were much more familiar with the players. We knew what they looked like from pictures in the papers and hockey cards.

I used to listen on a small plastic radio set on a little table between my brother's and my beds. I would punch up my pillow, hunker down in the blankets and listen. Foster was a poet. His voice had a cadence and urgency that matched the ebb and flow of the action. He called the players' names as if they were gods, as of course they were to us: Teeder Kennedy, Tod Sloan, Sid Smith. We understood hockey so well and Foster was so good at play-by-play broadcasting, there was no need for pictures. For thousands of us, it was pure magic. It's still one of my fondest childhood memories. I once wrote Foster to tell him.

A generation earlier, my father was lacing on his skates in Saskatoon. Two of his brothers also played hockey, and his father coached the team. My favorite snapshot of him is in full hockey gear, glaring straight-on into the camera. Except for the wear and tear on the uniform, it looks as if it was taken for a hockey card and helped me fantasize that I came from a great hockey family like the Hannigans or the Prentices.

My dad remembers year after year hauling water from the big water tank at the railway siding across town in buckets to flood the rink. His father finally had the bright idea to move the rink down to the rail yards.

The Prairies contributed more than their share of hockey players. There were never any thaws once the sloughs froze over and no shortage of road apples to play with. The ponds and riverbeds across Manitoba, Saskatchewan and Alberta were alive for seven months a year with the unmistakable sounds of hockey.

The boys from North Battleford, Medstead, Saskatoon and Moose Jaw, Sask., would soon be heard from. As would Canada in international hockey. We would come to be the country to beat. The Russians, the Swedes, the Czechs and the Germans all took dead aim at us and defined their progress in the years to come by how they measure against our teams. But why would a sport like hockey, with such fierce bodily contact, such violent action, such aggression at its core, come to be so much a part of a nation of supposedly easygoing, phlegmatic people?

Does it tell us anything about ourselves or is it merely because the sloughs and the ponds freeze early here and stay frozen a long time? Could it all be a matter of conditions and circumstances?

Perhaps a bit of that.

But we've had heated gymnasiums as long as anyone else, and you don't see the nation come to a standstill when our basketball team is playing the Soviet Union on television.

No, hockey is our game. And, like it or not, that says plenty about the Canadian character.

This is a macho game. A game of broken teeth, chipped bones, charley horses and worse. It's a game of strength and speed, where you go into the corners expecting to get hurt at least a little bit and maybe a lot. But if you want to play, you do it. Hockey players get a chuckle when baseball players talk about playing through their injuries. Being hurt in hockey is a given. You hurt every time you play.

It's a game of fierce checking, where tenacity and persistence pay off, where jabbing and poking and constant harassment get results; and those who wait for the breaks wait forever. Effective hockey doesn't have to be pretty. Ugly and mean can win the day. Hard work and giving no quarter are rewarded.

This is a game where size and strength mean something. Being powerful enough to stay on your feet in front of the net and knock the other guys down first will earn you a big salary. It's a game you can play at the professional level even if all you can do is remain upright on skates while you throw a good punch.

At its worst, it's a game of clutch and grab, of overly padded bodies sprawled on the ice, of awkward motion and desperate, ungainly attacks. It can be so disorganized and chaotic, even in the majors, to be funny. It can be violent enough to scare children and make adults ill.

That doesn't sound like a good microcosm of Canada. And it isn't, of course, because hockey is much more than that.

It's also a game of poise, balance, precision and much subtlety. It is a game that can be dominated by a relatively little fellow like Wayne Gretzky, because he has all those things plus astonishing athletic skill, inhuman anticipation, freaky peripheral vision and a lot of intelligence.

It's a game that at times is a work of art. Think of Jean Beliveau and Guy Lafleur skating with such power and beauty they could be ballet dancers. See Lafleur, like a spider, gliding over the ice hardly seeming to touch it, a 100-pound heart in a 170-pound body. Remember Beliveau, so classy at centre for Les Canadiens he could have played in a tux.

It is a game of breathtakingly beautiful images.

Frank Mahovlich in full flight down the left-wing boards, the puck cradled so gently on his stick, cutting at the blue line toward the net, the easy stride so deceptive the defensemen are still turning to face him as he glides by, the shift first right, then left, leaving the goalies long gone and the net open for a little flip into the corner. Frank looking embarrassed because it was all so easy.

Dave Keon in a Toronto Maple Leaf uniform in the playoffs staggering over the blue line so tired all he wants is off the ice, his face white and drained, his knees buckling, reaching down somewhere to find the energy to slap the crispest, cleanest shot of his career for a goal that wins it all.

Wayne Gretzky playing 40 of the 60 minutes for the Edmonton Oilers, his long hair damp and sticking to his neck, doing whatever it takes to keep his team in there. The night I'm remembering, he scored three goals and assisted on two in a 5-4 victory. In the post-game interview, he said it was a team effort and thanked his line mates for playing so well.

A little boy on a frozen pond just outside Cold Lake, Alta., skates until his legs tremble and the sun goes down, shoots a rock-hard tennis ball time after time into the snowbank, dreams his dreams and waits for his mother to call him home.

Sounds Canadian to me.